THE
GOSPEL
OF
ADVENT

Devotional Readings
from Christianity Today

2021

Editor: Kelli B. Trujillo / Design Director: Sarah Gordon / Designer: Cassandra Bauman /
Illustrator: Nicole Xu

CONTENTS

"I bring you good news . . ."

LUKE 2:10

With these words, the angel began a stunning gospel proclamation: The Savior, the promised Messiah, the Lord, had been born! When we think of the *gospel*—of the *Good News*—we rightly think of Jesus' death and resurrection. We think of our sin, of Jesus' sacrifice, of the salvation and eternal life Christ offers. In this sense, it's only natural to think of Easter as the "gospel" holiday—it marks the central events that make our redemption possible.

But in this devotional resource, we invite you to consider what the season of Advent can teach us about the Good News. Many core tenets of the gospel reverberate powerfully throughout Advent's traditional readings and themes. In Advent, we reflect on the mystery of the Incarnation, on Christ's purpose as the long-awaited Messiah, on our sin and need for repentance, on God's promises of salvation and justice, and on our firm hope in Christ's return and everlasting kingdom. We prepare to celebrate the "newborn King" who was "born that man no more may die," as Charles Wesley's beloved carol declares. And we're reminded again and again throughout Advent that the gospel is not just for us, but it is a message of "great joy for all the people" (Luke 2:10)—it's good news that's meant to be shared.

As you read and reflect on God's Word each day during these four weeks of Advent, our hope is that you engage with core truths of the gospel afresh and that, like the shepherds who encountered the Christ child, you glorify and praise God for all the things you hear and see (v. 20).

Kelli B. Trujillo, Editor

CHRIST'S RETURN & ETERNAL REIGN

This week, we focus on the Second Advent:
our sure hope in Christ's return. We explore
Scripture's portrayal of Christ's power and
righteous judgment, and the glorious future
we await with God in the new creation.

Read Titus 2:11–14 & Revelation 1:7–8

We wait for the blessed hope–the appearing of the glory of our great God and Savior, Jesus Christ.

TITUS 2:13

The End

KELLI B. TRUJILLO

We begin at the end. Not at the manger. Not with the Magi offering gifts of worship or the shepherds rejoicing in wonder. Not with Mary's visit to Elizabeth or Joseph's angelic dream. We begin not with Christ's First Advent, but with his Second.

Like a mixed-up storybook with the chapters all out of order, the season of Advent—and indeed the entire Christian liturgical year—starts with the end.

It's not a tame, pleasant, "they all lived happily ever after" ending. It's beautiful and fearful, awesome and terrifying. It's an ending that expands far beyond the limits of our human comprehension: *He will come again in glory to judge the living and the dead, and his kingdom will have no end.*

Advent begins with the eschaton: with Christ's power and glory, his righteous judgment, his ultimate victory and eternal reign. It shocks us out of our sentimentality about Christmas, inviting us into the far grander and more expansive story of the cosmos, in which the incarnate God who was laid in a manger and went to the cross will one day sit on the throne, and every knee will bow and every tongue confess he is Lord (Phil. 2:6–11).

Like Isaiah's response to his vision of God's holiness, our only natural response to contemplating the wonder and glory of Christ's second coming is to say, "Woe is me! I am a person of unclean lips" (Isa. 6:1–5). As we ponder Christ's holiness and power, we're drawn to our knees in repentance and humility. And like Thomas in his encounter with the risen Christ, we too proclaim, "My Lord and my God!" (John 20:28).

The Second Advent makes plain that to follow Jesus means to surrender all to his lordship in obedience and worship. We respond to Christ's promised return—"the blessed hope"—with a longing and anticipation that shapes our lives in the here and now, as we say "No" to the temptations of sin and live as people who are "eager to do what is good" (Titus 2:11–14).

When we begin at the end, Advent startles us in just the right way: jolting us out of our comfortable Christianity and familiar discipleship and drawing us into deeper repentance, devotion, and hope. When we start with this eschatological vision, we can then rightly approach the manger—for we know that there, wrapped in swaddling clothes, is the Savior whose glorious return is indeed our blessed hope, "our great God and Savior, Jesus Christ."

Read Titus 2:11–14 and Revelation 1:7–8.

(Option: Also reflect on Philippians 2:6–11.)

How does Christ's future return shape your life in the here and now? As you contemplate Christ's return, judgment, and reign, how do you desire to respond?

9

$$\frac{11}{29}$$

Read Luke 21:25–36

At that time they will see the Son of Man coming in a cloud with power and great glory.

LUKE 21:27

Watch and Pray

RACHEL GILSON

The second coming of Jesus will be in no way subtle. The totality of creation, from the heavens down to the roaring seas, will spasm; the totality of the peoples of the world will see and despair. There will literally be nowhere to hide, nowhere to find safety from the One who will finally come to bring justice. Nowhere, except in him who comes again to judge the living and the dead. While the nations will anguish, the followers of Jesus are told not to duck and cover, but to stand and lift their heads. Because they have hidden themselves in Christ seated in heaven, they need have no fear when he returns to earth.

Jesus wanted his disciples to understand that this event would come quickly and surely. There is immense debate about who "this generation" is (Luke 21:32). Perhaps it refers to Jesus' immediate listeners, for whom the fall of Jerusalem would be a sign and type of the coming end. Perhaps it means the generation who will see the signs of the coming, meaning that Christ's return will shortly follow these metaphorically sprouting leaves. Either way, Jesus promises that the event is more firm than the natural world itself.

What are disciples to do in the meantime—in the waiting? Those of us from certain church backgrounds may expect a call to evangelize and disciple others because people must know about this coming calamity. And yes, we must. Those of us from other church backgrounds might expect a call to practice justice because we are called to love the things God loves and hate what he hates. And yes, we must.

However, in this specific moment in Luke 21, Jesus called his disciples to be careful, to watch. The suddenness and ferocity of the end make a springing trap the appropriate image. Who is so arrogant to assume they will escape? The mundane temptations of wild partying or undue apprehension are both examples of how any human heart can be weighed down. And a heavy thing, carrying heavy burdens, cannot quickly enough jump out of the way.

Neither escapism nor worry can deliver what they promise. The first doesn't make reality go away; the other doesn't truly prepare us. Jesus calls us instead to watch and to pray. To pay attention, completely reliant on the God who is truly coming. Jesus wants his disciples to be able to stand before him then; he will answer that prayer.

Reflect on Luke 21:25–36.

What emotions or reactions does this passage stir up in you? How does it convict or inspire you? What does it emphasize about Jesus and the gospel? Invite Jesus to help you obey his call to watch and pray.

$$\frac{11}{30}$$

Read Matthew 25:31–46

The King will reply, "Truly I tell you, whatever you did for one of the least of these brothers and sisters of mine, you did for me."

MATTHEW 25:40

Right or Left?

RACHEL GILSON

In Matthew 24–25, Jesus teaches about his return and uses several parables to describe what "the kingdom of heaven will be like" (25:1). Perhaps the most unsettling element of Jesus' teaching in 25:31–46 is the surprise of both groups who are being judged. They don't protest about being judged per se; after all, the Son of Man has come in glory, attended by an immense gathering of heavenly beings, and even his throne is glorious. This entrance confirms and conveys his authority to judge. He has the right to call every nation before him, and come they must.

The surprise is not about the fact of judgment nor the rights of the judge. Instead, both those on the right and on the left are confused about the evidence. The sheep are looking at this King of glory and thinking, *Surely we would have known if we had served him. He is unmistakable.* The goats were thinking the same, but in reverse. When would they ever have refused such a one? They couldn't think of an instance.

In response, the glorious Christ reveals the key: He has always been identified, unified, with his brothers and sisters. This is more than mere affiliation; it is true identification. Who are his brothers and sisters? Jesus taught plainly, "Whoever does the will of my Father in heaven is my brother and sister and mother" (Matt. 12:50). No matter a person's station, ethnicity, gender, or nationality, if they are united with Christ, then caring for them is caring for Jesus himself.

This is not works-righteousness, where each person gets a reward or punishment based on his or her deeds. This is a revealing of allegiance to or rebellion against King Jesus—which is why there are only two destinations.

It would be easier, perhaps, to obey the *glorious* Christ—because we'd see his power with our own eyes. But God calls us to faith, not sight. In fact, at Christmas, we remember that he came almost in disguise. Even today, he is identified with his frail and foolish people.

Lip service won't do. Real trust in Jesus moves our allegiance to him and results in obedience. Do we believe him that service to lowly and despised Christians is better proof of our discipleship than even miracles and prophecy (7:21–23)? That we can't have the greatest commandment without the second, nor the second without the first (22:37–40)? The true allegiance of all will be revealed; let us put our faith in him.

Ponder Matthew 25:31–46.

(Option: Also read 7:21–23 and 22:37–40.)

How does this teaching about Christ's return and judgment shape your understanding of what it means to know and follow Jesus? How does the idea of true allegiance challenge you in your own daily discipleship?

12
01

Read Revelation 21:1–6

He who was
seated on the
throne said,
"I am making
everything new!"

REVELATION 21:5

All Things New

RICHARD BAUCKHAM

How have you coped with the pandemic? What has it done to your relationship with God? Some people have drawn closer to God and found the strength to get through difficult times. But for some, who perhaps lost loved ones or who shuddered at the scale of the suffering worldwide, the pandemic raised questions.

How can a loving God allow such things to happen? It's the age-old "problem of suffering"—at least as old as the Book of Job. The Bible has no single answer to it; instead, it gives us several different angles on it.

Then right at the end of the Bible, we find this message: " 'There will be no more death' or mourning or crying or pain" (Rev. 21:4). God is going to heal his creation of all that spoils and damages it.

People sometimes complain that there isn't much evidence of God's love in the Book of Revelation. Some might say the same of the pandemic. But can you imagine a more beautiful image of the love of God than this: God "will wipe every tear from their eyes" (v. 4)?

Revelation certainly does not stint in its portrayals of the horrors of history. But hope runs through it all and blossoms in this final vision that the prophet is given. God will make all things new. God has a new future for his whole creation.

When we think about the future, we most often think of where the past and the present will lead. But this is different. As only God can create, only God can renew his whole creation. It started with the resurrection of Jesus—one new thing that changes everything. In lives transformed by the Spirit of Christ, we have a foretaste of the new future.

That future itself goes far beyond what we can imagine. But John's vision invites us to also raise our eyes to that high mountain (v. 10) where the New Jerusalem comes down from heaven. With his eyes we can look much farther than we normally can see.

At the heart of the new future is God: "God's dwelling place is now among the people, and he will dwell with them. They will be his people, and God himself will be with them" (v. 3). This has always been God's purpose for his creation, and it is what will make all the difference.

Sharing John's vision is not just pious daydreaming. It gives us hope to live by. We can start living toward what God promises, and that will make all the difference to our lives now.

Meditate on Revelation 21:1–6.
How does this passage speak to pain and hardship in your life? In the world? How does it orient your spiritual perspective? Respond to God in a prayer of worship and trust.

Read Revelation 21:9–22:5

The city does not need the sun or the moon to shine on it, for the glory of God gives it light, and the Lamb is its lamp.

REVELATION 21:23

City of Light

RICHARD BAUCKHAM

When I moved from England to live in Scotland, one thing I found difficult was the shorter periods of daylight in the winter. On dull days, it could seem like it never got light at all. I found this mildly depressing, but some people are seriously affected by it and have to sit with lamps that imitate sunlight. We are all dependent on sunlight for our physical health and our mental well-being.

It is not surprising that in many cultures people have worshiped the sun, and sometimes the moon, too. Why does a sunny day lift our spirits? Why do many people love to bask in the sun? Science confirms that our planet's distance from the sun, with the light and heat that it provides, is essential to life on earth.

In this creation, God's blessings are mediated to us through creaturely means, sunlight among them. In the new creation, we shall live in God's immediate presence, immersed in it as we now are in daylight—and there will be no night.

Imagine it: a city filled with light. Imagine it like a brilliant crystalline jewel (Rev. 21:11), the light reflected in all the precious stones of many colors listed in verses 19–20. Imagine, if you can, the way the light shines through the transparent gold of which the city is made (vv. 18, 21).

Get a view of the city from a distance. It stands atop a mountain (v. 10) and shines out over all the surrounding country. It is the sunlight of that world. It is the light by which people live (v. 24).

Think, now, of a stained-glass window in a church with vivid depictions of biblical or other figures. The window itself is beautiful enough at all times, but when the sun shines through it, it *glows*. Its intense colors light up! In the New Jerusalem, the loveliness of all God's creatures will be a delight for all. We shall see them in their true colors. The light of God's immediate presence will not cancel out their shapes and colors, their created reality, but it will light them up, transfiguring them.

All through the Bible, light is a symbol of God and of Jesus (who said, "I am the light of the world" in John 8:12). Think about the ways God's light shines already into our lives in this world—how it lights up our lives, how we can walk in that light. If we see the light now, it will light up the path we can walk to the city of light. What can we take with us to present to God and to contribute to the life of that eternal city (Rev. 21:24, 26)?

Contemplate
Revelation 21:9–22:5.

What strikes you most about this beautiful imagery? What truths do the descriptions of shining light and illuminating glory convey about God? About the new creation? About our ultimate hope?

$\frac{12}{03}$

Read Revelation 22:12–20

"Surely I am coming soon." Amen. Come, Lord Jesus!

REVELATION 22:20, NRSV

Come, Lord Jesus!

RICHARD BAUCKHAM

The Bible ends with the prayer: "Come, Lord Jesus." It is a prayer that is echoed in many of our Advent hymns, such as "O Come, O Come, Emmanuel" and "Come, Thou Long Expected Jesus."

Christians have prayed it from the earliest days; it is the oldest Christian prayer we know (not counting the Lord's Prayer). We know this because Paul quotes the original Aramaic version, *Maranatha*, meaning "Our Lord, come!" (1 Cor. 16:22). For Paul to expect his Greek-speaking readers in Corinth to recognize this Aramaic phrase, it must have had a key place in early Christian worship.

In Revelation 22:20, it is a response to Jesus' promise to come. In verse 12 and again in verse 20, Jesus himself says, "I am coming soon." This promise runs through the whole Book of Revelation (see 2:5, 16; 3:11; 16:15; 22:7, 12, 20), promising judgment for some and blessing for others, until at last it evokes an answer: "Come!"

We hear that answer first in verse 17. It is the prayer of "the Spirit and the bride." By "the Spirit," what is probably meant is the Spirit speaking through Christian prophets in worship. The bride is the church as she joins this prayer of the Spirit.

We can picture the bride waiting for the Bridegroom to arrive. She is adorned and ready for him (see 19:7–8). The bride is not the church as such, but the church *as she should be*, expectant and prepared for the Lord's coming. She is the church that prays, "Come, Lord Jesus!"

We must imagine the Book of Revelation being read aloud in Christian worship. When the reader read the next sentence, "Let everyone who hears say, 'Come!'" (22:17, NRSV), the whole congregation would join in the prayer, shouting, "Come, Lord Jesus!" Their heartfelt prayer identifies them as the bride of the Lamb.

But in the second half of verse 17, the use of the word "come" shifts. Now it is the hearers, "everyone who is thirsty," who are invited to "come" and receive from God "the water of life" (NRSV). The water of life belongs in the new creation (21:6) and the New Jerusalem (22:1). But it is available already in the present to those who are awaiting the coming of Jesus.

It is as though he comes to us already, ahead of his final coming, and gives us a foretaste of the new creation. For that is what salvation is. We wait for him because we have met him already.

Reflect on Revelation 22:12–20.

What does it mean to pray, "Come, Lord Jesus"? How does this prayer challenge or change you? Join Christians around the globe and through the centuries as you pray this ancient prayer today.

12
04

Read 1 Thessalonians 3:9–13

May he strengthen your hearts
so that you will be blameless and
holy in the presence of our God
and Father when our Lord Jesus
comes with all his holy ones.

1 THESSALONIANS 3:13

The Gospel Life in Person

MATTHEW D. KIM

Have you ever missed someone badly and wanted to see them again? Over these long, seemingly endless months of the pandemic, there are many loved ones we've been unable to see, greet, and hug in person. Zoom and Face-Time simply don't cut it. We desire to be in the same space, same room, same place. We long to see them face to face.

The Apostle Paul also yearned to see the Thessalonian believers in person. He is overjoyed at Timothy's report of confidence that they were embodying the gospel, living it in action, by "standing firm in the Lord" (3:8). He desires to visit in person and yet this letter must suffice for now. What is his message to them? That the Good News must be lived out in person until we see Jesus face to face. What does this look like? The same Good News of Jesus' love is to "increase and overflow for each other and for everyone else" (v. 12).

This type of love is not easy to embody in our divided world. Many today have allowed worldly values to creep in and supplant Christian love and gospel witness. We may be more divided as a church than ever before.

This timely reminder from Paul to increase and overflow in love for others is not something we can achieve on our own.

Rather, Paul says, "May the Lord make your love increase" (v. 12).

The implications of the gospel are lived out through our Christ-like love, particularly for those we consider to be in the "everyone else" category. We cannot claim that we eagerly wait to see Jesus at the Second Coming—the consummation of the gospel story—when we can't stand the sight of our brothers and sisters in the Lord today!

As we await Jesus' return, Paul urges believers to "be blameless and holy" (v. 13) in a society that celebrates compromise and sin. Our hopeful anticipation of the Second Coming challenges us to always pursue holy lives to the glory of God. This includes bearing with one another and being patient with those with whom we disagree, relying on God's power to do so.

Paul urged the Thessalonians to live this way in light of Jesus' return: to let their present discipleship be shaped by their future hope. Like them, we long to see Jesus face to face. Advent reminds us that one day we will. May we strive to be people of love and holiness in the meantime. Come quickly, Lord Jesus!

Consider
1 Thessalonians 3:9–13.

How does anticipation of Christ's return shape your daily life? How do you desire as you live out the gospel life in person? Pray, inviting God to strengthen your heart and deepen your love for others as you await Christ's return.

SIN &
REDEMPTION

John the Baptist played a crucial role in preparing people for the Messiah. This week, we consider what Scripture says about John's purpose. We reflect on how his teachings about sin and repentance can speak to our own lives of Christian discipleship.

12
05

Read Malachi 3:1-4

I will send my
messenger, who
will prepare the
way before me.

MALACHI 3:1

He Won't Leave Us Alone

JEN ROSNER

Today we read from the last book of the Old Testament, just before we flip the page into the first chapter of Matthew. The Israelites have returned from the Babylonian exile, the Jerusalem temple has been rebuilt, and yet their relationship with God is still . . . complicated.

The Book of Malachi is structured around a series of declarations by God, which are met by questions and accusations from the people of Israel. As these dialogues unfold, Israel's ongoing sin and rebellion are laid bare, as is the steadfast character of Israel's God. Our passage in chapter 3 is introduced by Israel's pleading for the God of justice to show up (2:17), and God's promise to send a messenger who will prepare the way of the Lord (3:1). After that, God himself will come to the temple. What a hopeful promise! The God who has chosen the Israelites as his treasured people will come, demonstrating anew his commitment to his people.

This hope, however, is given a sharp edge in the next verse. Yes, God is coming—but who can endure the day of his coming? God will not pat the Israelites on the back for their half-hearted temple service or refusal to honor God fully. Indeed, the God who is coming is like a refiner's fire and a launderer's soap, putting the Israelites on trial for their injustices and waywardness.

During Advent, as we await the birth of the Messiah and long for God's coming yet again, the yearning is palpable. Our world is broken, and we need a savior. But, like the Israelites, the savior we await may not be exactly as we expect. He may not pat us on the back either. Rather, our shortcomings will be laid bare, and we too will be called to repent and change our ways.

But this is precisely the point. Our God is not a God who leaves us alone and lets us be just how we are. He is a God who *changes us,* and this change can only come about through an awakening to the parts of our lives that are in desperate need of reordering. It is this reordering, this opening of ourselves to the refining hand of God, that will indeed draw us nearer to God and closer to the people we were made to be.

Let us be open to God entering into our lives, and let us embrace that God showing up may not look exactly how we may have imagined. What *can* be trusted is the goodness and gentleness of this great God, the God of faithfulness, the God who will not leave us alone.

Read Malachi 3:1–4.

Consider its meaning in several possible layers: its original historical and cultural context, John the Baptist's and Jesus' coming, and Christ's return. What does this prophecy reveal about God's character and love? Pray, inviting God's refining work in your life.

Read Isaiah 40:1–5

Comfort, comfort my people ... Speak tenderly to Jerusalem, and proclaim to her that her hard service has been completed, that her sin has been paid for.

ISAIAH 40:1–2

Comfort My People

JEN ROSNER

As we seek to gain insight on this beautiful passage, a window into its meaning for the Jewish community can help us better understand its context and significance. The Jewish people worldwide move through a weekly biblical reading cycle, similar to the Christian lectionary. The darkest weeks of the cycle fall in midsummer, leading up to Tisha B'Av, the saddest day in the Jewish calendar. It commemorates the destruction of both the first and second temple in Jerusalem. Tisha B'Av also marks numerous other tragedies throughout Jewish history. It is a day of fasting and mourning. The Book of Lamentations is read publicly and Israel's sin before God is laid bare.

But that is not the end of the story. Immediately following Tisha B'Av, the reading cycle enters seven weeks of consolation, leading up to Rosh Hashanah, the Jewish New Year. Isaiah 40:1–26 is the designated reading for the week after Tisha B'Av, offering a reminder that judgment is not the final word. Each year, the Jewish people walk through the darkness of divine rebuke and are then reminded that God's grace and forgiveness ultimately carry the day. They emerge from a time of ashes and despair into a new promise of God's unyielding love.

Isaiah wrote during the expansion of the Assyrian empire and the demise of the kingdom of Israel (and eventually Judah). It was a tumultuous and tragic time, which Isaiah paints with haunting imagery. Yet Isaiah knew that this would not be Israel's ultimate destiny. His description of restoration is equally visionary, instilling hope and perseverance in a battle-sieged people who doubted God's presence in their midst.

Isaiah's words also point forward to the pinnacle of divine revelation in the New Testament and the role played by John the Baptist, who's identified as "one calling in the wilderness" (Matt. 3:3). The reference to Jerusalem's hard service being completed and her sin being paid for (Isa. 40:2) would one day become true for all nations, as Jesus proclaimed that all people on earth are now invited into a covenantal relationship with God.

The contours of this new covenant inaugurated by Jesus' life, death, and resurrection mirror the covenant Israel had long known. While there are repercussions for sin, God's forgiveness and commitment to his people are renewed again and again, like waves crashing on a shore. May we press into the comfort of God's presence and promises as we await the full revelation of his glory, even as Isaiah prophesied.

Contemplate Isaiah 40:1–5.

(Option: Also read vv. 6–26.)
How does the context of tragedy and sorrow—in the Jewish scriptural reading cycle and in Isaiah's day—enrich your reading of this passage and the comfort it offers? How might it deepen your understanding of John the Baptist's purpose?

Read Luke 1:67–79

You will go on before the Lord to prepare the way for him, to give his people the knowledge of salvation through the forgiveness of their sins.

LUKE 1:76–77

The Rising Son

WESLEY HILL

In my branch of the church, we pray the words of the song of Zechariah each day during the service of Morning Prayer. As the new day begins, we say or sing: "The sunrise shall visit us from on high to give light to those who sit in darkness and in the shadow of death, to guide our feet into the way of peace" (vv. 78–79, ESV).

Anyone who has taken the trouble to get up early and climb a hill or tower to watch the burning cusp of the sun swell into a cheering, blazing ball on the horizon will know how easy it is to treat a sunrise as a metaphor for hope. The rising sun says, "Whatever happened yesterday, here is a day of new possibilities. There is life beyond darkness and peace beyond strife."

Maybe the most famous use of the metaphor comes from the Old Testament prophet Malachi, who pictures the sun as a peaceable bird whose flight path showers mercy on those who look up to see it. In Eugene Peterson's memorable paraphrase, Malachi 4:2 reads, "For you, sunrise! The sun of righteousness will dawn on those who honor my name, healing radiating from its wings" (MSG).

What we hope for when we say these words morning after morning is that the sun's warm light would simply remind us of God's light that shines in our hearts with fresh grace for the day ahead (2 Cor. 4:6).

One of the things that's always a bit jarring to me, though, when I pray the song of Zechariah is that the somewhat gauzy, universally recognizable symbol of the rising sun sits side by side with a stubbornly concrete reference to a specific child from history: the cousin of Jesus, the one we know as John the Baptist. "You, my child," sings Zechariah, breaking away from his grandiose imagery to focus on one particular human being, "will be called a prophet of the Most High; for you will go on before the Lord to prepare the way for him" (Luke 1:76).

What this means for my prayer life, I've come to think, is that all the beautiful but somewhat underdetermined talk about divine light, health, peace, and so on comes into sharp focus in the events surrounding one particular first-century Israelite prophet who would one day, pointing away from himself, declare about Jesus: "Look, the Lamb of God, who takes away the sin of the world!" (John 1:29). The sun is meant to remind us of hope, yes—but, particularly, the hope of the Son himself.

Meditate on Luke 1:67–79.
What is God drawing your attention to in Zechariah's prophecy? What does this song emphasize about God? About humanity? About John's purpose and God's plan?

29

Read Luke 3:1–6

The word of God came to John son of Zechariah. . . . He went into all the country around the Jordan, preaching a baptism of repentance for the forgiveness of sins.

LUKE 3:2-3

Repentance Made Possible

JEN POLLOCK MICHEL

We're tempted to imagine the ancient world of the Bible as far more foreign than familiar. In phrases like, "In the fifteenth year of the reign of Tiberius Caesar" (Luke 3:1), we hear the yammering of our high school history teacher. But Luke's gospel introduces us to a recognizable world. A world where lust for power, celebrity, and wealth reigned supreme. In this world, political might made right. In AD 19, for example, Tiberius Caesar exiled the Jewish community from Rome—because he felt like it. In this world, religious loyalties were corrupted by political compromise. Archaeologists believe they may have found Caiaphas's house—its multiple stories, water installations, and mosaic floors all bearing witness to the high priest's coziness with the ruling party. Much like ours, this world was waiting for rescue.

John the Baptist may have been a member of one of the small holiness communities that fled Jerusalem because of the corruption. From the wilderness, John preached his "baptism of repentance for the forgiveness of sins" (v. 3) and announced a loud cry of salvation (v. 6). As the forerunner of Jesus, John was making a way for people to see what Rome, despite its promises, could never provide.

In the Jewish imagination, repentance was a means for restoring the blessing of God. Although repentance reminded people of their sin, it was nevertheless emphatically good news. We see this clearly in the book of Deuteronomy. As Moses reprised the terms of the covenant God made with Israel, he reminded God's people that sin would always be their ruin. To their own peril, he said, they "invoke a blessing on themselves, thinking, 'I will be safe, even though I persist in going my own way'" (29:19). But despite the pleasure people may think sin affords, it is always cause for eventual catastrophe—as Israel learned the hard way.

Repentance is a call to turn *from* our sin and turn *toward* God. To say it differently, repentance is a call to turn from self-harm and turn toward self-preservation. Repentance is a lifesaving measure.

But as the message of John reminds us, this turning is only made possible because God sent a "word . . . to John son of Zechariah in the wilderness" (Luke 3:2). The good news announcement is that God himself has prepared the way for God's people to return to him. During Advent, we remember that repentance is made possible because God enfleshes a Word—and sends him to speak, to serve, to save.

Consider Luke 3:1–6.
How is John's emphasis on repentance essential in preparing the way for Jesus? When have you experienced repentance as "a lifesaving measure"? Pray, inviting God to deepen your understanding and practice of repentance.

31

$$\frac{12}{09}$$

Read Luke 3:7–18

Produce fruit in keeping with repentance.

LUKE 3:8

Good, Severe News

JEN POLLOCK MICHEL

John the Baptist's blazing sermon of repentance is not the "ABC gospel" of many evangelical churches. John doesn't want people to simply *admit* their sin, *believe* in Jesus, and *confess* their faith in him. According to the Baptizer, repentance initiates life change. Love the poor! Be honest! Conduct your business with integrity! There's no tolerance here for religious dabbling. To sign up for John's baptism was to submit oneself to spiritual and moral *cleansing*, and according to Luke, these were words of "good news" (v. 18)!

Obedience to God had always been central to Israel's calling. Their family status was not dependent on their religious performance. Rather, their identity as God's treasured possession provided the foundation for their vocation of obedience. Through Abraham's family, God's people would represent God in the world: his holiness, his mercy, his steadfast love, and his faithfulness. "You will be for me a kingdom of priests and a holy nation," God told Moses before giving the Ten Commandments (Ex. 19:6). But Israel failed that calling, falling into idolatry and being cast from the Promised Land.

Even though God's people eventually returned to the land, the Roman occupation still signaled exile. So when John spoke of repentance, of *return*, it brought to mind God's blessings and their calling—and crowds flocked to hear.

The enthusiastic response to John's caustic language seems surprising. The Baptizer is no slick televangelist. His sermon text doesn't soothe with platitudes. It doesn't peddle moral evasions or play loose with God's "coming wrath" (Luke 3:7). It says clearly: Each of you is guilty of sin, and sin will be judged. Given our self-esteem culture, we might wonder who would have signed up for this spiritual straight talk. But, as anyone knows, if cancer is eating your lungs, you want it found and cut out. Or, as John the Baptist would say, spiritual health isn't possible without an ax (v. 9).

There's love in this warning, compassion in this severity. There's also hope beyond self-effort. God was sending another Baptizer (v. 16) who would make true repentance possible. "If I am told, over and over, to repent, to change, to orient my life to God, nothing will ever happen," Fleming Rutledge writes in *Advent*. "I don't need to hear exhortations to repent. I need power from outside myself to make me different." When the Messiah would come, he would baptize his followers by his Spirit—and leave none of them the same.

Reflect on Luke 3:7–18.
How is John's confrontational message "good news"? What might you need to heed in John's words? Pray, asking the Holy Spirit to work within you, producing fruit in your life that reflects repentance.

Read Matthew 3:1–12

In those days John the Baptist came, preaching in the wilderness of Judea and saying, "Repent, for the kingdom of heaven has come near."

MATTHEW 3:1-2

Amazing, Cleansing Grace

JEN POLLOCK MICHEL

The Gospel writer Matthew preserves the historical setting for John the Baptist's ministry with a simple timestamp: "In those days" (v. 1). To read the previous chapter (as well as Luke 3) is to understand these were the days of megalomaniacal rulers—like Herod the Great who, in bloodthirsty rage, killed the little boys of Bethlehem. After Herod died and his son had risen to power, Joseph remained afraid for his family and moved them to Nazareth "so that what was spoken by the prophets might be fulfilled, that he would be called a Nazarene" (2:23, ESV).

Matthew's gospel is insistent upon the fulfillment of God's prophetic promises. "God said—and it was accomplished," Matthew emphasizes over and over again. This notion isn't to be treated as self-evident, of course, not when visible reality suggests evil is winning. When babies are dead at the hands of an evil king, for example, can we really trust that heaven is breaking in, as John preaches (3:2)?

John the Baptist cuts the figure of Elijah in the Old Testament, dressed in camel's hair, eating locusts and wild honey. Elijah was another prophet who ministered under an evil regime. King Ahab, like Herod, also killed for ambition. After Elijah's dramatic victory over the prophets of Baal, his Queen Jezebel put a price on Elijah's head.

Repent, for the kingdom of heaven is at hand. This is essentially the word preached by all of God's prophets, and by God's grace, it is a word that arrives in the darkness. It's a word of good news: *There's been a change of administration.* This proclamation, preached both by John and Jesus, anticipates that another king will ascend to the throne. As the prophet Isaiah himself declared many hundreds of years earlier, the government of this king, unlike the government of King Ahab or King Herod, will be one of peace (Isa. 9:6–7).

To follow King Jesus is not simply to be *saved* by him; it's to be *changed* by him. According to Paul, the gospel tells us that Jesus "gave himself for us to redeem us from all wickedness and to purify for himself a people that are his very own, eager to do what is good" (Titus 2:14).

We know the working of amazing, saving, *cleansing* grace when God's people turn from sin and surrender themselves wholly to God. If Advent is the dawning of light, repentance is the daily habit of walking in it.

Contemplate Matthew 3:1–12.

How does the idea that the kingdom "has come near" (v. 2) or "is at hand" (ESV) add context to John's call to repent? What does this statement reveal about Jesus? How does it enrich your understanding of the gospel? Of cleansing grace?

35

12/11

Read John 1:29–34

John saw Jesus coming
toward him and said,
"Look, the Lamb of God,
who takes away the sin
of the world!"

JOHN 1:29

Behold the Lamb

ANTHONY J. CARTER

The Old Testament is replete with shepherds. Abraham was a shepherd, as were Jacob and Rachel, as well as Moses, King David, and the prophet Amos. Shepherding was an important job because the community of God's people in the Old Testament needed sheep. They needed lambs, a lot of lambs, in order to fulfill the requirement of sacrifices to God.

The thought of a seemingly endless slaughter of lambs can be unsettling for us. Just imagine how unsettling it must have been for those who participated in these bloody offerings! Yet because of sin, God required a sacrifice. He required a lamb. But not just any lamb. The lamb had to be spotless, without blemishes or defect (Lev. 22:21–22). In other words, it had to be perfect.

Even though God's people were tasked with choosing the most perfect lambs, those lambs were never perfect enough. Their sacrifice covered sin, but they could never actually take it away (Heb. 10:4). Every cry of a lamb sacrificed in the Old Testament was in some ways a cry of longing for the truly perfect Lamb of God.

This cry continued through the generations until one day, John the Baptist saw Jesus walking toward him and declared, "Look, the Lamb of God, who takes away the sin of the world!" (John 1:29). Here, John the Baptist offered an answer to the piercing question Isaac had asked his father Abraham many years before, and that echoed through the centuries: "Where is the lamb?" Abraham had replied to Isaac, "God himself will provide the lamb" (Gen. 22:7–8).

There by the river, John the Baptist declared Jesus to be the lamb God promised to provide. *Behold, the perfect, unspotted, unblemished Lamb of God* (see 1 Pet. 1:18–19).

We're not looking for the lamb anymore. He has come. Jesus Christ is that lamb who was sacrificed—crucified—in our place (1 Cor. 5:7). He is the lamb "pierced for our transgressions" and "crushed for our iniquities" (Isa. 53:5). Jesus is the lamb, the only lamb, that once and for all made the sacrifice for our sins (Heb. 10:12).

John bore witness to the fact that Jesus was the "God's Chosen One" (John 1:34). The baby who was born, whom John declared, was also "the Lamb who was slain" (Rev. 13:8). Today, when we worship the Lord, may we echo John's prophetic words: *Now behold the lamb!*

Read John 1:29–34.
(Option: Also reflect on John 1:6–8; 1 Cor. 5:7; 1 Pet. 1:18–19.)

How do John's teachings about sin and repentance connect with his testimony about Jesus? How do you desire to respond to Jesus as you contemplate his identity as the Lamb of God?

SACRIFICE
&
SALVATION

---

*God spoke through the prophets in the Old Testament,
using poetic words and imagery, to describe the hope
of salvation. This week, we contemplate prophecies
pointing toward the Messiah—the servant, the light,
the promised one God's people longed for.*

$$\frac{12}{12}$$

Read Isaiah 52:13–53:12

He was despised and rejected by mankind, a man of suffering, and familiar with pain.

ISAIAH 53:3

The God Who Suffers

HANNAH KING

During Advent, it is easy to sentimentalize the Incarnation. We imagine the God-man as a baby with his mother; we anticipate his ministry as "Wonderful Counselor" and "Prince of Peace" (Is. 9:6). These are true aspects of Jesus' identity and humanity, and are certainly appropriate scriptural themes for this time of year. But Isaiah's prophetic words in this last of his Servant Songs—which describe a coming servant of the Lord who will be found faithful to lead the nations—augment our understanding of Christ's incarnate life: Jesus was born to suffer and die.

Jesus' path to glory was not straightforward. Instead of being accepted by the world, he was despised and rejected (53:3). Instead of being exalted as king, he was tortured and murdered (53:5, 9). This is not merely a human tragedy—it is mysteriously part of the divine plan (53:10). Christ's voluntary suffering reveals his willingness to be not only our High Priest, but also the sacrificial lamb.

This profound reality is more than a theological concept. Jesus suffered as a human being in a physical body, sharing in the most painful and dark aspects of the human experience. He knows what it is to be brutalized and humiliated (52:14), oppressed and abandoned (53:8). In the Incarnation, Jesus identifies with us even in our worst forms of suffering. For those who experience the holidays as painful or lonely, this aspect of Jesus' life can be strangely comforting. No human tragedy extends beyond his understanding or his solidarity.

But Isaiah also makes it clear that Jesus' story does not end in suffering and death. Rather, his affliction is the means through which he achieves his victory: "After he has suffered, he will see the light of life and be satisfied" (53:11). This is more than personal vindication. As God's righteous servant, Jesus establishes justice and redemption for the nations of the earth. In other words, Jesus shares in our suffering so that we can share in his resurrection. His wounds redeem our own and become the very source of our healing (53:5).

As we contemplate the Incarnation in all its beauty, we can also be thankful for its grit. Jesus came down from heaven and then went further still: to the very depth of human shame and suffering. He did this for our sake. And when we meet him in our own suffering, sin, and shame, we can be confident that he will not leave us there—for by his wounds we are healed.

Meditate on Isaiah 52:13–53:12.

What draws your attention most? How does this poetic prophecy deepen your engagement with gospel? Pray, reflecting on how these dark descriptions of what the servant would suffer are crucial in our observance of Advent.

$$\frac{12}{13}$$

Read Isaiah 11:1–5 & Jeremiah 33:14–16

A shoot will come up from the stump of Jesse; from his roots a Branch will bear fruit. The Spirit of the Lord will rest on him.

ISAIAH 11:1-2

What Hope Looks Like

MARLENA GRAVES

I have three daughters, and I often consider them in wonder. I simply cannot wrap my mind around how whole worlds—my daughters' lives and identities and futures—are generated from a microscopic, fertilized egg. How is the miracle and mystery of human life possible? God only knows.

From the prophet Isaiah's time on down through Jeremiah's time, generations of Israelites in the northern and southern kingdoms experienced destruction of their land, lives, families, and livelihoods as God's judgment for their sins. All hope for a good outcome was lost. Too many generations had experienced death in a thousand different ways for them to believe their circumstances would turn out any differently. And yet they still ached for a savior to rescue them, for a messiah to snatch them from the clutches of their enemies.

When hope vanished, when they were living as oppressed aliens in empires of destruction, the prophet Isaiah and later the prophet Jeremiah both spoke hope. Through them, God communicated this promise of hope, described as a tiny shoot coming "up from the stump of Jesse," like a "righteous Branch" sprouting from "David's line" (Isa. 11:1; Jer. 33:15).

Generations passed before God's promised hope appeared. And yet fulfill his promise he did, through the advent of our Lord Jesus Christ. As generations of God's people wondered if God would ever show up, at just the right time, Jesus came. Jesus, who is "Our Righteous Savior" (Jer. 33:16), the one on whom the Spirit rests, the one full of righteousness and justice.

In his humanity, Jesus sprang from the divine seed entrusted to Joseph and Mary. Jesus: a tiny shoot sprouting from the stump of Jesse who contains all worlds and possible worlds—for in him and "through him are all things made" and "in him all things hold together" (John 1:3; Col. 1:17). Again, I pause in wonder, in awe.

Just as I cannot fathom the nature of my daughters' miraculous existence, I cannot fathom the mysteries of God's salvation or the whos, whats, wheres, and whys of God's timing. But I do know that God keeps his promises—in history, to his people, and to individuals. God always shows up. Always. He shows up when we least expect it and in ways we don't expect—when all hope seems lost. Indeed, our God shows up like a tiny green shoot in a forest that has been burned to the ground. Watch for it.

Contemplate Isaiah 11:1–5 and Jeremiah 33:14–16.

What hope do these passages offer? What might the original recipients of these prophecies have thought or wondered? Pray, reflecting on the sprouting shoot of hope and salvation God promised for his people.

$$\frac{12}{14}$$

Read Isaiah 12:2–6; 52:7–10 & Zephaniah 3:14–20

"At that time I will gather you; at that time I will bring you home. I will give you honor and praise among all the peoples of the earth when I restore your fortunes before your very eyes," says the Lord.

ZEPHANIAH 3:20

Bringing Us Home

MARLENA GRAVES

When you hear *home*, what comes to mind? For some, the word triggers trauma. Others feel ambivalent toward their notions and memories of home. Some are itching to get away from home. Others never felt at home. And, of course, there are many who are deeply fond of home, who cannot wait to get home. Many who'd even consider themselves "homebodies."

It is part of the human condition to long for home—for a place where we belong. A place where we can be ourselves, where we are known and loved, and where we feel, well, *at home*. Home is to be a place of peace, where we are at ease instead of on guard. Home is safe. Ultimately, in some sense, all of us long to be homebodies—to be strangers to alienation.

In Zephaniah 3:20, the Lord says, "At that time I will gather you; at that time I will bring you home." God promises to one day bring home his people all throughout the world. It is a home of feasting and singing because of all God has accomplished through his salvation (Isa. 52:9, 10). It is a home of regular, free-for-all, spur-of-the-moment flash mobs of celebration. It is a party for the ages because what is too good to be true *is* true (Zeph. 3:14–15). It is full of glee and praise. It is a place of refuge, where God is our "strength and defense" (Isa. 12:2). In this home, it is a level playing field where the lowly, the oppressed, and the exiles return to the place they feel most themselves (Zeph. 3:19–20). In each of these passages, God was speaking to a particular people in a particular time and place. But these prophecies also expand beyond their immediate context, for coming home is part and parcel of salvation itself.

Jesus echoes these sentiments about home when he proclaims, "Anyone who loves me will obey my teaching. My Father will love them, and we will come to them and make our home with them" (John 14:23). And earlier, in John 14:3, Jesus tells us that he is preparing a place, a home, just for us.

We are a home to God, at home in God, and God is preparing a home for us. But not just in the bye and bye; here and now we can find a semblance of home and be God's home to others. We can "bring good news" and invite others to join us (Isa. 52:7). Who wouldn't want to be in such a home?

Reflect on Isaiah 12:2–6; 52:7–10; Zephaniah 3:14–20.
How do these prophecies expand your vision of salvation and what it means, and what Jesus came to offer? How do you desire to bring this good news of home to others? Pray, expressing your gratitude and worship to God.

Read Isaiah 42:1–7

I will … make you to be a covenant for the people and a light for the Gentiles, to open eyes that are blind, to free captives from prison and to release from the dungeon those who sit in darkness.

ISAIAH 42:6–7

True Hope

KRISTIE ANYABWILE

Sometimes we forget that we are idol makers. We cling to the idols of power, wealth, pride, other people, institutions, misinformation, tradition. And sometimes we also forget that God is not silent in the face of idolatry and evil. He exposes their empty promises and reveals Christ as the remedy for our idol-making tendencies.

In Isaiah 42, God responds to the empty idolatry and meaningless false gods he addressed in the previous chapter by announcing the coming of his servant in whom he delights, and chose, and in whom his Spirit dwells. While idols are weak and powerless, God's promised, faithful servant will bring forth justice to the entire world. He will not tread on the vulnerable or boast in pride. Instead, his tender compassion will be shown toward those who are weak, hurting, or whose faith is faltering.

So much is happening in our world today that can cause us to question where God is when the attraction of idols deludes even the most faithful among us, when injustice envelops our world like a dark cloud, and when the weak can barely breathe because their cries for relief have rendered them weary. This passage reminds us that the promised servant will one day take all that is wrong with the world and make it right. He's chosen by God to bring justice in humility and love. He's called by God to be a covenant for his people, the blameless agent to carry out the word and will of God.

In Matthew 12:15–21, after Jesus has healed many people who were part of a large crowd that followed him, the Word tells us that "this was to fulfill what was spoken through the prophet Isaiah" in Isaiah 42:1–4. All the promises of God reside in Jesus and have their fulfillment in him (Matt. 5:17; 2 Cor. 1:20). Jesus embodies truth, justice, righteousness, faithfulness, humility, meekness, and every fruit of the Spirit. And for all who call him "Lord," through our union with him, our lives are to reflect the same—albeit imperfectly. For only Jesus has the power to bring the nations out of darkness and into his marvelous light. Only Jesus can set prisoners free from sin and darkness.

As we reflect this Advent season on God's faithfulness to send his servant, may we remember that while justice was ultimately served on the cross, it is also a future reality that we long for as we await the Second Advent.

Ponder Isaiah 42:1–7.

(Option: Also read Isaiah 41.)
What draws your attention in this description of the servant? How does Jesus fulfill these promises—and how *will* he? In prayer, confess ways you've placed hope in contemporary idols. Ask God to help you place all of your hope in him.

$$\frac{12}{16}$$

The Lord has anointed me to proclaim good news to the poor. He has sent me to bind up the brokenhearted, to proclaim freedom for the captives and release from darkness for the prisoners.

ISAIAH 61:1

The Messiah's Mission

GLENN PACKIAM

Debates frequently arise about the mission of the church. Are we supposed to evangelize or work for justice? Should Christians prioritize the forgiveness of sins or the care of the sick? These debates have deep roots in an old divide about both theology and mission. Broadly speaking, one group might be immovable about feeding the hungry but indifferent about the Virgin Birth; the other might be the reverse. One may give themselves to improving the world and the other to the promise of a heavenly afterlife.

Both sides of this divide would have been rebuked by Jesus. When he went to the synagogue and read from Isaiah 61, he announced his mission. The Spirit of the Lord had anointed him to bring "good news to the poor . . . to proclaim release to the captives and recovery of sight to the blind, to let the oppressed go free, to proclaim the year of the Lord's favor'" (Luke 4:18–19, NRSV throughout). Jesus demonstrated how the kingdom of God brings forgiveness and freedom, healing and hope—all signs of the renewal of creation to come.

Isaiah himself looked ahead to the day when God would bring about a new heavens and a new earth where "all flesh" would come and worship (Isa. 66:22–23). Though Isaiah and Israel with him would have imagined it happening in one move, God in Christ—the Anointed One!—was inaugurating a reign that will one day culminate in the remaking of the world. He will start with us—with the God-human relationship that was at the heart of creation. And he will work through the justified to bring justice. The "set right" people join God in his work of setting the world right.

But in announcing the fulfillment of Isaiah's prophecy, Jesus was also pointing to himself as the kingdom-bringer. This was no mere social improvement project. The total overhaul of the world and its systems would begin with a seed falling to the ground and dying (John 12:24). The Messiah alone inaugurates the kingdom.

The mission of the Messiah, the Spirit-Anointed One, continues through the Messiah's people—the little anointed ones. Luke parallels this story in his second volume by talking about the Spirit anointing the followers of Jesus in the upper room. In a very real sense, the mission of the church is not really the mission of the church but *of the Messiah*. It is Jesus who started it; Jesus who by the Spirit empowers us to participate in it; and Jesus who will come again in glory to bring his reign to its culmination.

Read Isaiah 61:1–4, 8–11.

(Option: Also read Luke 4:14–21.)

Consider Isaiah's original audience: What hope did this promise give? What did it emphasize about God's character and plans? What stands out to you today as you read this promise in light of Jesus and the gospel?

Read Isaiah 9:1–2

The people walking in darkness have seen a great light; on those living in the land of deep darkness a light has dawned.

ISAIAH 9:2

The Light is Coming

RICH VILLODAS

I won't soon forget a short text message exchange I recently had with a friend from out of town. He was doing the whole NYC tourist thing. I asked him for an overview of his itinerary. He responded via text: "first stop is to the 9/11 memorial." Reading those words put me in an immediate, unforced state of reflection.

You see, although I'm a native New Yorker, I've never been to the 9/11 memorial. It's not that I don't know how to get there. It's just … well … *darkness*. I'd have to face the darkness of that day and be reminded of the ongoing manifestations of darkness that pervade our world—the wars, the racism, the loss and fragile nature of life. So much darkness.

Yet, with all the darkness before us, Advent situates our world within a larger, more hopeful story. It's the story of God's overpowering light among his people. A light that illuminates the individual and collective darkness we experience and witness. A healing light.

Advent invites us into a prayerful expectation, a holy waiting, an attentive gaze. What are we awaiting? Resplendent light. God's light.

Isaiah announces that a great light is coming—coming from an unexpected source. It's making its way through a child, the Messiah. This light is not to be found in some new political power, or in some cultural movement. It's not located in a particular ideology, but rather is found through the living-God-in-flesh. This is an important theme in Scripture, picked up by John, the Gospel writer. In John's words, the light that has come is not some impersonal electromagnetic radiation. It's the staggering truth of the personal manifestation of God's very self in Jesus Christ. Jesus is the light that shines in the darkness, and the darkness has not overcome it (1:5).

Isaiah prophetically speaks about a day that would be coming—a day that has already come in Jesus. Yet we also await another day when the darkness will be fully and finally overpowered. This is the promise in this season.

Advent reminds us that no matter how dark it gets, the light has come, and the light is coming. So be of good cheer! The darkness you feel today will not have the last word. Neither will the grief, uncertainty, and despair. As Wendell Berry once said, "It gets darker and darker and darker, and then Jesus is born."

Contemplate Isaiah 9:1–2.

(Option: Also read Matthew 4:12–17 and John 1:1–5.)

What darkness in this world or in your life is sometimes difficult to face? How does Isaiah's promise encourage you? How has Jesus—the Light—overcome darkness in your life?

51

$$\frac{12}{18}$$

Read Isaiah 9:6–7

For to us a child is born,
to us a son is given, and
the government will be
on his shoulders.

ISAIAH 9:6

The Baby King

MATTHEW D. KIM

I n my experience, watching cartoon movies has been an essential part of being a dad to three young boys. *Boss Baby* is one such movie. The film caricatures an infant who's "all grown up" and constantly bossing around his seven-year-old brother behind their parents' backs.

The irony in Isaiah 9:6–7 is a similar juxtaposition: a newborn baby who is "all grown up." Isaiah describes this promised one as a newborn child, a government ruler, and the "Wonderful Counselor, Mighty God, Everlasting Father, Prince of Peace."

The amazing testimony of this prophetic text is that Jesus is all of this, and so much more. Jesus, born as a human child, was both fully human and fully divine: the God-Man, the Baby King.

Isaiah was speaking to a discouraged Jewish community that had been groping in darkness, hoping to find a pathway to freedom from their "distress and darkness and fearful gloom" (8:22). Into this context, Isaiah prophesies, "He will reign on David's throne and over his kingdom, establishing and upholding it with justice and righteousness from that time on and forever" (9:7) This reference to David's throne hearkens back to God's promise to David: "I will raise up your offspring to succeed you … I will establish his kingdom…. I will establish the throne of his kingdom forever" (2 Sam. 7:12–13). God is a covenant-keeping God. And nothing will stand in the way of this promised miracle: "The zeal of the Lord Almighty will accomplish this" (Isa. 9:7). God is *zealous* to keep his covenants with his people.

God is also zealous and passionate about the gospel. The Good News of Jesus becoming flesh is that in Christ there is no longer darkness (Isa. 9:2; John 1:4–5, 14). God is on the move, across the globe, on every continent, in every nation, exposing the darkness through the power of Christ's first coming and his imminent return. Jesus' incarnational entry into the world signifies a new day, "for to us a child is born, to us a son is given" (Isa. 9:6)!

This is the Good News, the gospel, that we must share with the world. The light has come; the light is Jesus! We no longer need to live in darkness and we can share this light with a world that needs to hear about our "Mighty God," our "Prince of Peace." May we proclaim it freely: *Jesus, the Baby King, is here, and he wants to reign in your hearts.*

Meditate on Isaiah 9:6–7.

(Option: Also reflect on John 1:14.)
In what ways does this promise point toward core tenets of the gospel? Which aspects of this prophecy most draw your attention? Why? Pray, praising Christ for each aspect of his identity described in Isaiah 9:6–7.

INCARNATION & NATIVITY

This week, we step into the events of the Nativity
and consider the miracle of the eternal Word
entering the world as a human child. We learn
lessons of faith from the people whom God chose
to play a part in these events. And we celebrate
the good news of great joy for all people!

$$\frac{12}{19}$$

Read Philippians 2:5–11

Though he was in the form of God, [Jesus] did not regard equality with God as something to be exploited, but emptied himself, taking the form of a slave, being born in human likeness.

PHILIPPIANS 2:6–7, NRSV

What It Means to Be God

WESLEY HILL

One common way of understanding the beautiful hymn of praise to Jesus Christ in Philippians 2:5–11 is that it shows us an utterly incomprehensible paradox: The mighty Son of God, who, together with his Father, brought creation into being, subsequently deigned to become a lowly human being—the equivalent of a powerful monarch being reduced to a scuttling beetle.

This way of reading Philippians 2 emphasizes the mismatch between the Son's pre-incarnate glory and the humiliation he underwent during his earthly life. The little word *though* in most English translations has been the vital clue for this interpretation: "*though* he was in the form of God, [Jesus] did not regard equality with God as something to be exploited, but emptied himself, taking the form of a slave, being born in human likeness" (vv. 6–7, NRSV throughout, emphasis added). *Despite* sharing equality with God the Father, *nevertheless* Jesus the Son chose to give up that status for us.

That's a plausible interpretation of Paul's words, certainly. But the original language is ambiguous, and it's possible to translate it differently, leaving out the contrastive connector *though*. Paul might easily have meant something subtly different: *because* he was in the form of God, *therefore* Jesus emptied himself.

In the first way of reading it, there's something fundamentally incommensurate between the Son of God's glory and his self-emptying. The former is understood *in spite of* the latter. And there's obviously much truth in that way of interpreting Paul's words, which underscores for us the cost God agreed to pay in order to draw near to us.

But in the second way of reading Paul's hymn, there's something mysteriously *congruent* between the eternal splendor of God's Son and his voluntary self-abnegation in the Incarnation. The latter reveals or explains what the former is really all about, and it turns out that God's character is self-giving love "all the way down," so to speak.

In other words, if we want to understand what Jesus the Son's equality with God the Father really means—what it looks like when it's translated into the form of a human life—then we should look to that tiny baby on Mary's breast, that forlorn figure on the cross of Calvary, and that tenderhearted gardener who speaks peace to his friends that first Easter morning. By living for us, dying for us, and rising for us, Jesus not only reveals true humanness to us—he shows us what God's deity fundamentally amounts to.

Consider Philippians 2:5–11.

(Option: Also reflect on John 1:14.)
How does the Incarnation point us toward deep truths about the love and nature of God? How are these truths central to the gospel? How do they impact your daily life? Pray, expressing your response to God.

$$\frac{12}{20}$$

Read Luke 1:5–25, 57–66

Your wife Elizabeth will bear you a son, and you are to call him John.... He will go on before the Lord, in the spirit and power of Elijah ... to make ready a people prepared for the Lord.

LUKE 1:13, 17

Silent Time, Holy Time

JONATHAN T. PENNINGTON

If you grew up with snow at Christmas, you know there's nothing quite like the silence of a cold winter night. This is not just a sentimental idea—it's part of God's creational design. Fresh snow absorbs and dampens sound. Father Joseph Mohr was one such man who reflected on the phenomenon of a cold winter night. Mohr was the young priest who penned the words that became the beloved carol we often sing this time of year, "Silent Night."

In the backstory to Jesus' birth, we meet another priest, Zechariah, and his wife, Elizabeth. Luke tells us that they were both of priestly descent and were faithful and godly people. But they also suffered greatly—their long marriage had been childless and they were now old. Then a miracle happened: The angel Gabriel told Zechariah that God would answer their decades-long, anguished prayers. They were going to have a son!

This story could end there, and it would be a delightful Christmas tale of sadness being replaced with joy. But there's an unexpected and dark note in the tune that we can't ignore. Because Zechariah struggled to believe Gabriel's message (and who wouldn't?), he was struck mute for the entirety of Elizabeth's pregnancy. He was silent. Zechariah went from being a respectable, articulate priest of God to an old man who could only communicate with hand signals. This was humbling—even humiliating. What are we to make of this troubling turn?

God is always doing a thousand good things in every situation, even if we can't see them. God's heart of compassion is yet at work here in providing this old couple with a son of joy. God's power is manifested in eventually using this son to usher redemption into the world. He would become the famous baptizing prophet in the wilderness, calling God's people back and pointing ahead to Jesus.

The story of Zechariah shows us that God continues to do his good and gracious work even amid our brokenness and disbelief. Zechariah's stumbling faith was no hindrance to God's power. Though Zechariah's forced silence was frustrating and humbling, in reality, it was a gift. Through this negative miracle, God showed Zechariah and the world that these events were not mere coincidences. No, this silent season demonstrated that God was on the move in a new and powerful way to bring life into the world. As a result, Zechariah's story didn't end with judgment, but with God opening his mouth once again to proclaim the beauty of God's mercy.

Read Luke 1:5–25, 57–66.

(Option: Also revisit vv. 67–79.)

Zechariah was the first to learn God was doing something amazing—something God's people had been waiting for. What do you imagine Zechariah thought or wondered during his months of silence? What does his story highlight about God and salvation?

$$\frac{12}{21}$$

Read Luke 1:26–38

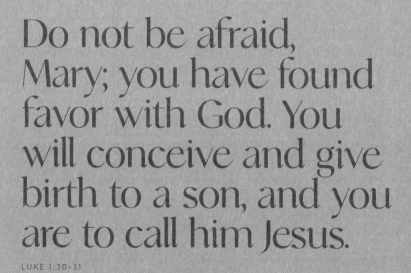

Do not be afraid,
Mary; you have found
favor with God. You
will conceive and give
birth to a son, and you
are to call him Jesus.

LUKE 1:30–31

Let it Be

GLENN PACKIAM

O bedience would be easy if it all made sense. And if we agreed. Or if we thought of the plan ourselves. But I suppose then it wouldn't really be obedience, would it?

When we read the stories of women and men of great faith, we imagine there was no struggle—that they heard the word of the Lord and rushed to obey right away. But the truth is, even when the word of the Lord is clear, obedience is challenging.

An angel of the Lord appeared to Mary. An angel! We might tell ourselves that if we were to have an angelic visitation, obedience would be easy—but we would be fooling ourselves. Mary, the Bible tells us, was "greatly troubled" (Luke 1:29). More than that, Mary had some serious questions. "Mary said to the angel, 'How can this be, since I am a virgin?' " (v. 34, NRSV). Fair point.

In many respects, Mary's question is not all that different from Zechariah's. When the angel told him that he and his equally aged wife were going to have a son, Zechariah asked, "How can I be sure?" (v. 18), also translated as "How will I know?" (NRSV). And yet Zechariah was struck mute.

We might parse the grammar of their respective questions and mine the language for clues, but I suspect the answer is not so much in the initial response as in their subsequent reactions. We have no reason to think Zechariah moved beyond bewilderment or disbelief during this initial encounter. (Though in time, of course, he did.) But in verses 26–38, Mary seemed to quickly move to a posture of surrender. "Then Mary said, 'Here am I, the servant of the Lord; let it be with me according to your word' " (Luke 1:38, NRSV).

Paul would later pray that Christ would be formed in us, Jesus' followers (Gal. 4:19). But it is Mary who *actually* had Christ being formed in her—in her very womb! While the Virgin Birth and the Incarnation are cornerstone miracles in Christian confession, we also find in this moment of Mary's a paradigm of spiritual formation. For Christ to be formed in us, like Mary we must move through our turbulence and uncertainty and doubt to the posture of surrender. Participation in Christ happens as we pray, "Here am I, the servant of the Lord; let it be with me according to your word." Even when we are tempted to fixate on "How can this be?", may God give us the grace to end up in the "Let it be" of faith.

Ponder Luke 1:26–38.

Why is it significant that Mary was initially "greatly troubled" and voiced a question? How does she exemplify spiritual formation here? How do you feel challenged or inspired by Mary's response? Pray, expressing your total surrender to God.

$$\frac{12}{22}$$

Read Luke 1:39–56

His mercy extends to those who fear him, from generation to generation.

LUKE 1:50

A Pregnant Promise

HANNAH KING

Mary's first recorded activity during her pregnancy was to visit her cousin Elizabeth. Both women were recipients of a miraculous pregnancy, and Luke links their stories so that we read them as a single narrative unit. This reminds us that the personal experiences of these two families are embedded in the same larger story of redemption.

Some see echoes of 2 Samuel 6 in Mary's visit to Elizabeth. There we read of the ark of the covenant residing in the hill country of Judea for three months; of David asking, "How can the ark of the Lord ever come to me?" (v. 9); and then David eventually leaping and dancing in its presence (see also Luke 1:39, 41, 43, 56). These similarities led many church fathers to view the ark of the covenant (which represented the presence of God) as in some ways prefiguring Mary (who carried the Son of God within her own womb). The presence of the Lord that once overshadowed the ark in the tabernacle (Ex. 40:35) had now come to rest upon a lowly virgin (Luke 1:35). Mary is honored throughout church history because the Incarnation began within her.

Mary received this blessing by returning blessing to God. Her song of praise expresses gratitude for God's favor (vv. 47–49), but immediately broadens in scope to describe God's mercy toward *all* who fear him (v. 50). She recapitulates many scriptural themes, illustrating that God's acts toward her are in continuity with the grand biblical narrative. God has not only done great things for one woman, but he has made good on his promise to rescue his people from oppression.

Mary's song was also prophetic. In declaring God's mighty acts, she exclusively used the past tense: *He has shown strength, he has scattered the proud, he has exalted the humble.* The arrival of Jesus guarantees God's victory. Even though we don't yet see it in fullness, God has already secured our salvation and the renewal of our world.

Though Mary's role is unique, she is a model for all Christians. We can emulate her worshipful, hopeful response to God's promises, even when they seem invisible. We can also remember her as an embodiment of the very promise she proclaims: the lowly will be exalted (vv. 48, 52). God chose her, a poor and unimportant girl, to carry the blessing and the presence of the Messiah. This privilege begins with Mary but belongs to all who fear God, to all who hunger and thirst for righteousness.

Contemplate Luke 1:39–56.

(Option: Also read 2 Samuel 6.)

What insights do you draw from the comparison of Mary and the ark of the covenant? How do Elizabeth's and Mary's reactions to these events speak you? Reflect on Mary's song, then express your own words of praise to God.

$$\frac{12}{23}$$

She will give birth to a
son, and you are to give
him the name Jesus,
because he will save his
people from their sins.

MATTHEW 1:21

Gospel Anticipation

MATTHEW D. KIM

W hen we think of the Christmas story, we often envision a nicely packaged, stained-glass image of little baby Jesus lying in a manger with Mary and Joseph serenely nearby. Yet the events leading up to Jesus' birth were far from neat. In fact, they were brimming with messiness and controversy. You can just feel the tension in Matthew's narrative voice in 1:18–19 as he describes Mary's pregnancy prior to their marriage and Joseph's contemplation of divorce.

We can imagine the extent of Joseph's shock—and perhaps even shame—regarding Mary's pregnancy. But then he, like Mary, was visited by an angel. Joseph responded to the angel's news with great humility and anticipation that this child to be born would "save his people from their sins" (v. 21). This news of salvation, too, would have been shocking—*wonderfully* shocking—for Joseph.

In our despondent world, there are times when the gospel message of salvation may lose its wow factor for Christians. We can easily take for granted that Jesus came to save sinners, which includes the unrepentant as well as the regenerate—in other words, *us*. This Advent and Christmas, may the shock of the highly anticipated event of Christ's birth (especially for Joseph and Mary) not lose its impact on us. May we wonder and marvel afresh at Jesus'

willingness to be the sacrificial lamb who came to save his people from their sins.

Matthew points out another detail that can draw us into wonder: In the birth of Christ Jesus, we witness a prophetic fulfillment of Isaiah 7:14: "The virgin will conceive and give birth to a son, and will call him Immanuel." Jesus is the Incarnation, Immanuel, who *is* "God with us" (Matt. 1:22–23).

During this season of global turmoil, the Incarnation of Jesus emboldens us in at least two ways. It can galvanize believers toward a deep-rooted faith in a Savior who indwells his people through the Holy Spirit. God is *with us*. We can live confidently and victoriously, not as victims but as victors in the Christian life.

And, for those of us who may have become apathetic in our faith, we are reminded that the gospel story generates vitality and purpose, especially for us to share this Good News with others. Jesus came as a helpless baby, but will come back as a just and righteous Lord at whose name every knee will bow and every tongue will confess (Phil. 2:10). May we share this Good News generously. The day of salvation is now.

Read Matthew 1:18–25.

Imagine these events from Joseph's perspective: What emotions or questions might he have wrestled with? How was his faith challenged and changed? Now consider your own perspective: How does this passage emphasize key truths of the gospel?

$$\frac{12}{24}$$

Read Luke 2:1-7

The time came for the baby to be born, and she gave birth to her firstborn, a son. She wrapped him in cloths and placed him in a manger, because there was no guest room available for them.

LUKE 2:6-7

Quietly Hidden

TRACEY GEE

Emperor Augustus issued a sweeping decree for all in the Roman world to be registered in a census. Many of us are familiar with this detail in the story of Jesus' birth because it's what brought Mary and Joseph to Bethlehem—in fulfillment of the prophecy in Micah 5:2–5a. But it's also notable because it demonstrates Augustus's considerable power as emperor. He says the word, and all must take notice. There was no option to ignore him.

Unlike the emperor, Jesus was easy to miss. His birth, which was prophesied and long awaited, contrasts sharply with Augustus's power. Jesus was born in humble and obscure circumstances, easy to overlook. As the Gospel narrative develops, there are people who are able to recognize Jesus as God in their midst, but they are a select few. As it turns out, the Incarnation is something that's easy to ignore—and most do it without even knowing it.

If we want to be people who see and recognize the incarnate presence of God in our lives and our world, what do we do? It reminds me of a time I lost a contact lens in a large hotel lobby. I blinked, noticed an odd feeling in my eye, and before I knew it my contact lens had landed somewhere on the bright, patterned carpet.

I froze, searched, and tried to keep others from inadvertently crushing it. A couple of hotel staff members took pity on me and helped. To my relief, we finally found it quietly hiding underneath a nearby chair. That experience taught me that when you're trying to notice something that's easily missed, it helps to stop, look closely, and get others to help you.

What if we, as God's people, stopped and slowed down enough to look closely and take in the beauty of the Incarnation? The Word becoming flesh and entering our world as an infant in order to live "among us" is joyful news for a weary world (John 1:14)! But if we don't make the intentional choice to stop and look intently, we too might miss truly seeing Jesus, quietly hidden but present in each moment of our lives—a bit like a small contact lens unnoticed in the busyness of people on their way to something else.

What if we chose to cultivate an awareness of God's incarnate presence around us? And what if we helped each other to do that as community? May we long for the kind of lives that allow us to notice the Incarnation, to stop and see new life and hope, even when it appears in a manger.

Reflect on Luke 2:1–7.

(Option: Also read Micah 5:2–5a and John 1:1–18.)

What does the simple description of Jesus' birth in Luke 2:1–7 convey? How might it be surprising? How is it fitting? Pray, expressing your response to Jesus' humble birth and the beauty of the Incarnation.

12/25

Read Luke 2:8–20

Do not be afraid. I bring you good
news that will cause great joy for
all the people. Today in the town
of David a Savior has been born to
you; he is the Messiah, the Lord.

LUKE 2:10-11

Great Joy for All People

RACHEL GILSON

The overwhelming tone of this passage is *joy*. God had sent his Son to earth, and heaven's celebration spilled down to the world with praise and stunning glory. And to whom does the joyful announcement come? Not to the most glorious of humanity, but rather to the most normal, mundane, and even earthy. The text reeks of animals, from the sheep being watched by the shepherds to the feeding trough that cradled Jesus. Christmas is a stunning picture of the gospel: God did not abandon his creation, but went a great distance, at great cost, to personally redeem it.

Luke records a variety of responses to the proclamation. Understandably, the first feeling of the shepherds is fear as they are confronted by creatures so unlike themselves. But their fear was soon replaced by eagerness. After all, this first coming was not like the second will be. While the second coming of Christ will usher in the judgment of all, this first was an offer of joy to all people, which would result in true and lasting peace for those who responded to it (vv. 10, 14).

The shepherds' diligence to seek out the sign was rewarded with finding the family, just as the angels had said. But the shepherds did not keep the news to themselves. They were just as diligent in reporting what they had been told as they were in seeking out the child. This is the heart of gospel proclamation: hearing it for ourselves, experiencing that God has kept his word, and sharing the very good news of sure salvation with others.

Those who heard the shepherds' testimony were amazed (v. 18). This doesn't necessarily mean they comprehended the full gravity of what the angels had told the shepherds about the infant: Savior, Messiah, Lord. Perhaps, hearing only average shepherds (and not an angelic host) and seeing only a common newborn, the glory was too obscured for some. Yet God calls us to live by faith in him, not by sight.

Mary, for her part, took it all to heart, turning it over in her mind. And the shepherds rounded out their spontaneous missionary journey by praising and glorifying God. Christ the Lord, our Savior, took on human nature for us and came to be our peace. May our response today—like the shepherds—resound in joy, praise, and glory!

Read Luke 2:8–20.

Reflect on all you've read and considered during Advent. How do you desire to respond in praise to God? How might you, like the shepherds, share this Good News with others? Pray—and rejoice!

01
06

Read Matthew 2:1–12

They saw the child
with his mother Mary,
and they bowed down
and worshiped him.
Then they opened their
treasures and presented
him with gifts of gold,
frankincense and myrrh.

MATTHEW 2:11

A Light to the Nations

GLENN PACKIAM

Who is the Good News for? When we get deals and offers in the mail, they sometimes call their sale or promotion a "friends and family" special. Some things are too good to keep to yourself, but they're also too radical to open up to everyone. This marketing approach highlights how we're conditioned to think that if something is exclusive—if we some-how have insider status—it's valuable. And conversely, if it's universal, it's not.

That's what makes the birth of Jesus so shockingly revolutionary. It is the best news the world could receive: God had come to save his people! But this salvation was not just for the people with whom God had made a covenant. It was for everyone—all people, in all places, at all times.

We see an early glimpse of this in Matthew 2 and the contrast it draws between King Herod and the true Messiah, King Jesus. Herod infamously rose to power through political opportunism and brutality. When word was going around that a new king of the Jews was born in Bethlehem, Herod would do everything in his power—including killing innocent babies (vv. 13–18)—to protect the power he had schemed to gain.

But where Herod's story is about a rise to power, Jesus' is about a descent from power. There in the manger was the one who "did not regard equality with God as something to be exploited," who "emptied himself" for us (Phil. 2:6–7, NRSV). Where Herod lied and murdered to keep people away, Jesus in his infancy and early life was already *drawing people near*.

And not just some people, or even just God's covenant people. Matthew tells us about Magi—astrologers or philosophers or men of wisdom—who came from afar, bearing gifts for this child. The worship these non-Jewish visitors offered Israel's Messiah as they bowed down before him signals the expansive scope of God's promise. The Christ child would be "a light for the Gentiles" so that God's "salvation may reach to the ends of the earth" (Isa. 42:6; 49:6). In this scene from Jesus' early childhood, we see the global reach of the gospel: "Nations will come to your light, and kings to the brightness of your dawn" (Isa. 60:3).

Despite Herod's efforts to grasp at earthly power, there is only one King who at whose name every knee will bow (Phil. 2:10). Only one whose rule is Good News not for some, but for all. The Lord reigns—let the *earth* rejoice! Come and worship King Jesus!

Reflect on Matthew 2:1–12.
(Option: Also read Isaiah 49:1–6; 60:1–6; Philippians 2:6–7.)

Why is this early scene of Gentiles worshiping Jesus so significant? What does this scene convey about the Good News? How do you desire to respond to God?

IDEAS FOR FAMILIES & GROUPS

IDEAS FOR FAMILIES

- With teens or preteens, read and discuss the devotions together each evening. With younger kids, focus on just the Scripture passages and reflection prompts.

- Launch with a family discussion on this question: What is the gospel? Read the introduction (p. 5) and share that you'll be looking together for ways the themes and scriptural readings of Advent emphasize core aspects of the Good News. Then, throughout Advent, use different colored sticky notes to create a large "stained glass" window together on a sliding glass door or large window of your home. Each night, jot down notes about key gospel ideas or other responses to your readings and add them to the window.

- Print out the lyrics of Charles Wesley's "Hark! The Herald Angels Sing" and take time each week to discuss phrases in the hymn that connect with central ideas in the gospel and in the daily Advent readings. Sing the song together throughout Advent and Christmas.

WEEK 1

- Have each family member secretly pick a favorite book (such as a beloved picture book or a chapter book family members are familiar with). Give each person a turn reading aloud the last sentence of their book (without showing the book to the family) and then work together to guess which book it might be. Once you've guessed all the books, use this experience to talk about the way Advent begins at the end. Discuss: How does the end—Jesus' return and our hope of eternal life with him—impact our lives now?

- Ask: What are some things in life that upset you, are unfair, or make you feel angry or hopeless? (Option: Use newspapers or online news sites to generate ideas regarding current events.) Record on a posterboard some of the evils, injustices, and painful realities of life, like war, abuse, cancer, poverty, racism, stress, personal conflicts, and so on. Then tear up the poster together as you talk about our ultimate hope in Christ's future reign described in Revelation 21:1–5.

- Go outside to watch a sunrise together. Use the experience to talk about Zechariah's song in Luke 1:67–79 (and especially vv. 78–79). Discuss the ways Zechariah described John the Baptist's role and the image of the rising sun that points toward the coming of Jesus.

- Go on a family drive to look at area Christmas lights, but do it in a creative way. At each intersection, let a different family member make this decision: Will we keep going in the same direction or will we turn and go a different direction? At the end of the drive together, use the experience as an object lesson on repentance. As Jen Pollock Michel put it on p. 31, "Repentance is a call to turn *from* our sin and turn *toward* God." Repentance doesn't just mean saying "sorry"—it means turning and going in a different direction. Discuss why the call to repent is good news and emphasize God's generous forgiveness and grace.

WEEK 3

- Use a telescope or binoculars to look at far-off objects. Discuss how God used Old Testament prophets to see some of what God would do in the future. Talk about some of the truths the prophets foretold about Jesus.

- Turn off the lights in your house (other than Christmas tree lights) to play flashlight tag or flashlight hide-and-seek. Have fun together, then discuss Isaiah 9:2 and John 1:4–5, 9 and Christ's identity as the light promised in Isaiah 9.

WEEK 4

- Try this challenge: a family dinner without any talking. Communicate only with hand signals, facial expressions, and writing. Afterward, talk about the experience, imagining what Zechariah thought or felt during many months of silent waiting.

- Reflect on the shepherds' immediate response to seeing baby Jesus: telling others about him! Create a Christmas card as a family that tells about Jesus, then mail it to someone to share the Good News.

IDEAS FOR GROUPS

WHEN YOU MEET

To use this resource with your Bible study group, encourage members to read the daily Scripture passages, devotions, and reflection prompts, taking notes about their time in the Word. When you gather, select three to six of the week's Scripture passages and reflection questions to guide your discussion. In addition, select some of the activity suggestions below.

WEEK 1

- Say the Nicene Creed together, then discuss the line: "He will come again in glory to judge the living and the dead, and his kingdom will have no end." Do you think the church emphasizes these ideas enough in discipleship or evangelism? Why or why not? Why are these ideas so central in Christian belief? What role do these ideas play in your own understanding of the gospel or in your daily discipleship?

- Sing the hymns "O Come, O Come, Emmanuel" and "Come, Thou Long Expected Jesus" together. Discuss why the ancient prayer "Come, Lord Jesus" is so central to Advent. How could regularly praying this way impact a person's faith and daily life?

WEEK 2

- Put John's repeated charge "Repent!" into action by spending time in silent repentance and confession together. Option: Light a fire in a fireplace, then have group members privately write words, phrases, or symbols representing their confession on their own pieces of paper. To illustrate God's abundant and total forgiveness, invite group members to crumble up their confessions and toss them into the fire.

- Part of John the Baptist's focus was on emphasizing the importance of "fruit in keeping with repentance," and he specifically noted the importance of sharing clothing and food with the poor (Luke 3:8, 11). Decide on a simple way to put this charge into action as a group during the holiday season, such as volunteering at a food pantry together or collecting funds to provide clothing and other necessities to a local family in need.

- Listen to portions of Handel's *Messiah* together as you reflect on Old Testament prophecies foretelling the coming of Jesus.

- If your group meets in the evening, bundle up to go outside and look at the stars in the night sky. Read Isaiah 9:2 and John 1:5, then spend time specifically praying for those who do not know Jesus. Ask God to help your group share the gospel of light with those who may be in darkness.

WEEK 4

- Discuss the lyrics of Charles Wesley's carol "Hark! The Herald Angels Sing!" Draw out key phrases and ideas that resonate with central ideas you've discussed during Advent. Sing the song together as an expression of worship.

- Prepare plates of Christmas cookies or treats as a group, with each person identifying a friend or neighbor they'll give a plate of cookies to. Focus especially on those who may not know Jesus, and spend time in prayer for those people. Pray for future opportunities to share the Good News with them.

CONTRIBUTORS

KRISTIE ANYABWILE
is the editor of *His Testimonies, My Heritage* and the author of *Literarily: How Understanding Bible Genres Transforms Bible Study* (March 2022).

RICHARD BAUCKHAM
is senior scholar at Ridley Hall, Cambridge, and the author of many books, including *Who Is God?* and *Theology of the Book of Revelation.*

ANTHONY J. CARTER
is the lead pastor of East Point Church in East Point, Georgia. He is the author of several books, including *Dying to Speak* and *Running from Mercy.*

TRACEY GEE
is a leadership development coach and consultant. She is the author of *Mark* (Alabaster Guided Meditations) and a coauthor of *More Than Serving Tea.*

RACHEL GILSON
serves on Cru's leadership team for theological development and culture. She is the author of *Born Again This Way: Coming Out, Coming to Faith, and What Comes Next.*

MARLENA GRAVES
is a doctoral student and adjunct seminary professor. She is the author of several books, including *The Way Up Is Down: Becoming Yourself by Forgetting Yourself.*

WESLEY HILL

is a priest serving at Trinity Episcopal Cathedral, Pittsburgh, Pennsylvania, and an associate professor of New Testament at Western Theological Seminary in Holland, Michigan.

HANNAH KING

is a priest and writer in the Anglican Church in North America. She serves as associate pastor at Village Church in Greenville, South Carolina.

MATTHEW D. KIM

is the George F. Bennett Professor of Preaching and Practical Theology at Gordon-Conwell Theological Seminary and the author of *Preaching to People in Pain*.

JEN POLLOCK MICHEL

is a writer, podcast host, and speaker based in Toronto. She's the author of four books, including *A Habit Called Faith* and *Surprised by Paradox*.

GLENN PACKIAM

is an associate senior pastor at New Life Church in Colorado Springs. His books include *Worship and the World to Come* and *The Resilient Pastor* (February 2022).

JONATHAN T. PENNINGTON

is a professor of New Testament at Southern Seminary and a pastor of spiritual formation. His books include *Jesus the Great Philosopher*.

JEN ROSNER

is affiliate assistant professor of systematic theology at Fuller Theological Seminary and the author of *Finding Messiah: A Journey Into the Jewishness of the Gospel*.

RICH VILLODAS

is the lead pastor of New Life Fellowship in Queens, New York. He is the author of *The Deeply Formed Life: Five Transformative Values to Root Us in the Way of Jesus*.

Hail the heavenly Prince of Peace!
Hail the Sun of Righteousness!
Light and life to all he brings,
Risen with healing in his wings.
Mild he lays his glory by,
Born that man no more may die;
Born to raise the sons of earth,
Born to give them second birth.
Hark! The herald angels sing,
"Glory to the newborn King!"

"HARK! THE HERALD ANGELS SING"
BY CHARLES WESLEY, 1739